IOWA

BY ELAINE HADLEY

CONTENT CONSULTANT
Jeff Bremer, PhD
Associate Professor of American History
Iowa State University

Core Library
An Imprint of Abdo Publishing
abdobooks.com

abdobooks.com

Published by Abdo Publishing, a division of ABDO, PO Box 398166, Minneapolis, Minnesota 55439.

Printed in the United States of America, North Mankato, Minnesota.
052022
092022

THIS BOOK CONTAINS
RECYCLED MATERIALS

Cover Photo: Shutterstock Images
Interior Photos: Bella Bender/Shutterstock Images, 4–5, 45; Nancy Bauer/Shutterstock Images,
7; Red Line Editorial, 9 (Iowa), 9 (USA); iStockphoto, 10–11, 23, 31, 34–35, 43; Dennis Magee/
The Courier/AP Images, 12; John T. Bowen/Library of Congress, 14; Lukasz Stefanski/Shutterstock
Images, 17 (flag); Shutterstock Images, 17 (bird), 17 (flower); Yuriy Buyvol/Shutterstock Images, 17
(rock); Alexander Tolstykh/Shutterstock Images, 17 (tree); Ralf Broskvar/Shutterstock Images, 20–21;
Chris Boswell/iStockphoto, 25; Larry Lindell/iStockphoto, 28–29; Harris & Ewing/Library of Congress,
36; Lukun Zheng/Shutterstock Images, 39

Editor: Angela Lim
Series Designer: Joshua Olson

Library of Congress Control Number: 2021951410

Publisher's Cataloging-in-Publication Data

Names: Hadley, Elaine, author.
Title: Iowa / by Elaine Hadley
Description: Minneapolis, Minnesota : Abdo Publishing, 2023 | Series: Core library of US states |
        Includes online resources and index.
Identifiers: ISBN 9781532197567 (lib. bdg.) | ISBN 9781098270322 (ebook)
Subjects: LCSH: U.S. states--Juvenile literature. | Midwest States--Juvenile literature. | Iowa--History--
        Juvenile literature. | Physical geography--United States--Juvenile literature.
Classification: DDC 977.7--dc23

Population demographics broken down by race and ethnicity come from the 2019 census estimate.
Population totals come from the 2020 census.

CONTENTS

THE HAWKEYE STATE

People scream with excitement as they zip around on a roller coaster. A crowd sits and listens to a band perform. Vendors sell foods on sticks. Some of their creations include deep-fried hot dogs and hard-boiled eggs, each served on a stick. People marvel at a butter cow sculpture as they walk past.

This is the Iowa State Fair. It is held each year in Des Moines. The fair takes place for 11 days in the beginning of August. It's the

The Iowa State Fair has activities and excitement for all visitors.

THE BUTTER COW

One of the most famous parts of the Iowa State Fair is a cow made from butter. The fair's butter sculptor takes a frame made from metal, wood, and mesh and adds butter to shape the cow. The final product weighs 600 pounds (270 kg). J. K. Daniels sculpted the fair's first butter cow in 1911. Norma "Duffy" Lyon took over in 1960 as the fourth sculptor. She was the first woman. Sarah Pratt became the lead butter sculptor in 2006. In addition to the butter cow, Pratt makes other butter sculptures. She has sculpted Superman, Harry Potter, and other figures.

largest event in the state. More than 1 million people visited the Iowa State Fair in 2019. Visitors can try exciting foods, listen to music, and learn more about Iowa.

EXPLORING IOWA

Iowa is known as the Hawkeye State. This nickname may have come from a character in books by James Fenimore Cooper. Cooper is an American author from the 1800s. He wrote about exploring the early United States. The state's nickname may also honor Black Hawk, a Sauk leader. The Sauk were

The Mississippi River is 2,350 miles (3,780 km) long. It starts in Minnesota and empties into the Gulf of Mexico.

influential in shaping Iowa's history. Some of the Sauk still live in Iowa today as members of Meskwaki nation.

The Mississippi River forms Iowa's eastern border. The Missouri River forms the western border. Minnesota borders Iowa to the north. South Dakota and Nebraska are to the west. Wisconsin and Illinois are to the east. Missouri lies south of Iowa. Iowa is one of 12 states that make up the Midwest, a region located in the middle of the United States. Approximately 90 percent of

PERSPECTIVES

IOWA SPORTS

Iowa does not have any professional sports teams. But college sports are a big deal. Two of the state universities have a rivalry. The University of Iowa is in Iowa City. Its teams are the Hawkeyes. Iowa State University is in Ames. Its teams are the Cyclones. The Hawkeye and Cyclone football teams compete annually for the Cy-Hawk Trophy. The ESPN television show *College GameDay* was on location for the 2019 Cy-Hawk football game. Producer Drew Gallagher said, "I just think in-state rivalries are really cool for *GameDay*. . . . There's nothing like an in-state rivalry where your next-door neighbor might support the team that you hate."

Iowa's land is used for agriculture, such as growing corn.

But Iowa has more than just cornfields. The state's largest cities are Des Moines, Cedar Rapids, and Davenport. Des Moines is the capital. Cedar Rapids is known for large businesses. Davenport is part of the Quad Cities, a group of cities in Iowa and Illinois. From farms to cities, Iowa is home to many great people and places.

MAP OF
IOWA

Iowa has many important cities and landmarks. How does this map help you understand all that Iowa has to offer?

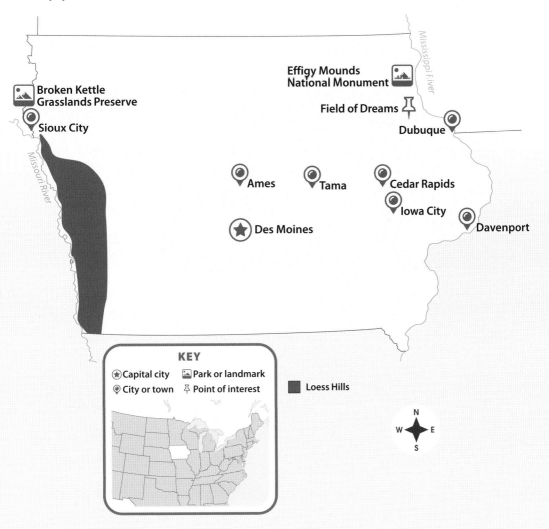

Mississippi River

Effigy Mounds
National Monument

Broken Kettle
Grasslands Preserve

Field of Dreams

Sioux City

Dubuque

Missouri River

Ames

Tama

Cedar Rapids

Iowa City

Des Moines

Davenport

KEY

⭐ Capital city   🏞 Park or landmark

◉ City or town   📌 Point of interest

■ Loess Hills

N
W   E
S

HISTORY OF IOWA

Historians believe Paleo-Indians first arrived in Iowa more than 11,000 years ago. These ancient peoples were the ancestors of today's American Indians. The first settlements in Iowa were built approximately 8,500 years ago. People began farming Iowa's fertile land approximately 3,000 years ago.

By the 1600s, the Dakota (Sioux) and Ioway were the dominant American Indian peoples in the Iowa region. During this time,

People have been growing crops in the Iowa area for thousands of years.

11

People from the Meskwaki Nation continue to celebrate their rich heritage today.

French fur traders arrived in what is now Iowa. The first people the French encountered were the Baxoje, whom they called Ioway. This later became the state name.

American Indian nations moved into and out of the state throughout Iowa history. The Sauk and the Meskwaki (Fox) were separate nations living in the Wisconsin region. They arrived in Iowa in the 1700s. The nations formed an alliance to fight the French. They became historically linked. Conflicts with the French and other American Indian nations in their homeland caused them to move. They moved into eastern Iowa and western Illinois.

In 1788 a French Canadian man named Julien Dubuque founded the first European settlement in present-day Iowa. He sought permission from the Meskwaki to mine lead near modern-day Dubuque. The city was named after him. Some historians identify Dubuque's wife as Potosi, a Meskwaki woman. A relationship of this nature would have helped build trust between the settlers and the Meskwaki.

LOUISIANA PURCHASE

In 1803 US leaders made a deal with the French. The deal was called the Louisiana Purchase. It added land west of the Mississippi

EFFIGY MOUNDS

Effigy Mounds National Monument is located in northeastern Iowa. People of early cultures created more than 200 earthen mounds in the area. The park was established in 1949 and covers 2,526 acres (1,022 ha). There are four kinds of mounds in the park. Effigy mounds are the most famous. Many of these mounds are in the shape of bears or birds. Historians don't know the exact purpose of the mounds. But some of them were burial mounds. Others were ceremonial. Twenty American Indian tribes and nations are culturally associated with the monument.

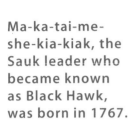

Ma-ka-tai-me-she-kia-kiak, the Sauk leader who became known as Black Hawk, was born in 1767.

to the United States. Part of this new land would become the state of Iowa.

After the Louisiana Purchase, American settlers in the eastern United States wanted to move farther west. The US government made treaties with American Indian nations. The treaties encouraged American Indian peoples to sell their homelands. Sometimes tribes were forced into signing the treaties.

In 1831 Sauk and Meskwaki leaders signed a treaty with the US government. The treaty gave up the peoples' lands east of the Mississippi River.

They would have to move entirely into Iowa. By the time these nations arrived in Iowa, it was too late to grow crops. Many of the Sauk and Meskwaki went hungry that winter.

The following year some Sauk and Meskwaki people returned to their traditional lands. They were led by Black Hawk, a Sauk leader. He hoped to use the land for farming. The US Army and Illinois militia chased Black Hawk and his followers from the land. Black Hawk attempted peace talks with the US Army, but misunderstandings led to conflict. This conflict was called the Black Hawk War. The Sauk and the Meskwaki were forced to give up more land in Iowa as a result of their defeat.

By the 1850s nearly all of the American Indian nations with traditional lands in Iowa had been pushed out of the area. Many of the Sauk and the Meskwaki were forced into Kansas. The Meskwaki Nation includes both the Sauk and the Meskwaki. On July 13, 1857, the Meskwaki Nation purchased 80 acres (32 ha) of land near Tama, Iowa. In the years that followed, many members of the Meskwaki Nation came back to Iowa.

SLAVERY AND STATEHOOD

Iowa became a territory in 1838. A US territory needed a population of more than 60,000 people before it could apply for statehood. By 1844 the territory had more than 75,000 people.

But another factor played into Iowa's statehood. At the time, slavery was allowed in parts of the United States. Iowa wanted to enter as a free state, where slavery was not allowed. The US government tried to maintain balance between free and slave states. This way neither group of states would have more power than the other in Congress. A slave state and a free state had to be admitted together.

Iowa became the twenty-ninth US state on December 28, 1846. It joined with Florida, a slave state. Iowa played a role in the Underground Railroad.

IOWA
QUICK FACTS

Iowa is home to many types of wildlife. Take a close look at the state symbols of Iowa. What do they show you about the animals and plants that live in the region?

Abbreviation: IA
Nickname: The Hawkeye State
Motto: Our liberties we prize and our rights we will maintain.
Date of statehood: December 28, 1846
Capital: Des Moines
Population: 3,190,369
Area: 56,273 square miles (145,746 sq km)

STATE SYMBOLS

State bird
Eastern goldfinch

State rock
Geode

State flower
Wild rose

State tree
Oak

This was a network of people that helped enslaved people escape slavery. Enslaved people could pass through Iowa while fleeing southern slave states.

PERSPECTIVES

FIRST FEMALE LAWYER

Arabella Mansfield, born in Iowa, was the first female lawyer in the United States. When she began studying at Iowa Wesleyan University in Mount Pleasant, women were not allowed to be lawyers. Still, Mansfield graduated in 1866 at the top of her class. In 1869 she became the first woman to pass the bar exam. Law students must pass this test to become lawyers. After Mansfield passed the exam, the Iowa Supreme Court ruled that women could practice law. It was the first state to allow women to do so.

IOWA'S GOVERNMENT

Iowa's state government has three main branches. The executive branch carries out laws. The state's courts form the judicial branch, which reviews laws. And the legislative branch makes the state's laws.

Iowa plays an important role in

US presidential elections. It holds the first caucus. The caucus determines which candidates in a party have the most supporters. Each candidate's supporters are counted. The candidate with the most supporters throughout the state is the caucus winner. Presidential candidates spend a lot of time and money on the Iowa caucus. The Iowa caucus can determine which candidates have enough support to continue running for president.

FURTHER EVIDENCE

Chapter Two discusses the history of treaties between American Indian nations and the US government. What was one of the main points of this chapter? What evidence is included to support this point? Visit the website below. Does the website support an existing piece of evidence in the chapter? Or does it offer new evidence?

WHAT VALUES SHAPED TREATY MAKING BETWEEN NATIVE NATIONS AND THE UNITED STATES?

abdocorelibrary.com/iowa

CHAPTER
THREE

GEOGRAPHY AND CLIMATE

owa's geography is mostly flat plains. The Mississippi and Missouri Rivers form the eastern and western borders of Iowa. Floodplains surround the rivers. This flat, wet land provides fertile soil. This soil helps plants grow.

However, Iowa is not all flat. Some areas feature rolling hills. The northeast is home to bluffs, rugged land, and limestone caves. In addition the Loess Hills lie along the Missouri River. The bluffs along the river stand 100 to

Hiking trails cut through the Loess Hills.

200 feet (30–60 m) high. Winds carved deep rifts into the sides of the bluffs.

Iowa has more than 70,000 miles (115,000 km) of rivers and streams. Fish such as bass, trout, pike, and carp swim in them. River otters live in all 99 of Iowa's counties. Forests grow along the riverbanks. Silver maple and cottonwood trees grow close to the water. Oak and hickory trees grow on higher land. These forests provide cooler temperatures for animals such as deer and beavers.

FOSSILS IN IOWA

Iowa looked much different 365 million years ago. Back then, Iowa was part of an ocean. Fossils from this period can be found throughout the state. The Fossil and Prairie Park Preserve in Rockford is one place people can go to find fossils. The fossils are usually of invertebrates. Visitors can keep the fossils they find.

PRAIRIE HOME

Beyond the forested riverbanks lie prairies and wetlands. More than 100 types of prairie grasses and wildflowers grow in

The regal fritillary butterfly is one animal that relies on Iowa's prairies to survive.

Iowa, including the wild rose. The wild rose is Iowa's state flower. Its deep roots help the plant soak up water from the ground. They also anchor the plants to the soil. Prairie plants are strong. They can survive harsh wind, freezing temperatures, and hot summers. And their roots keep soil from blowing away in the wind.

Prairies are home to all kinds of creatures. Birds and butterflies fly through the sky. Eastern goldfinches, cardinals, and blue jays can be spotted throughout the state. People may even see bald eagles.

Many plants and animals depend on prairies and wetlands. Wetlands provide places for birds such as geese and cranes to nest. And many birds rest in wetlands while migrating, including mallards.

Tall grasses and wildflowers thrive on the prairie. They give food and shelter to many animals.

However, the state's landscape changed as people cleared land for farming. Nearly 90 percent of its wetlands were drained. Prairies used to cover 80 percent of Iowa. Less than 0.1 percent of Iowa's prairie remains today.

Since 1975 Iowa's government has made laws to protect wildlife and help it recover. The laws protect some of the remaining wetlands and stop people from draining them. Some groups work to restore wetlands. People have planted prairie grasses too. The Broken Kettle Grasslands Preserve is the largest area of continuous prairie in Iowa.

CLIMATE AND FLOODING

Temperatures in Iowa change greatly throughout the year. Summers are hot and humid. July temperatures average 80 to 90 degrees Fahrenheit (27–32°C). Iowa winters can be extremely cold and snowy. The coldest

The high waters of the Mississippi River caused major flooding in Davenport in 2019.

temperature ever recorded in Iowa was −47 degrees Fahrenheit (−44°C). Iowa can see snow as early as September or as late as May.

Spring tends to bring the most rain. In an average year, Iowa receives 35 inches (89 cm) of rain. But sometimes it gets much more. Iowa's landscape makes it vulnerable to flooding. Heavy rains cause water to pool on the flat land. Melting snow and ice can also cause floods. When the ground is frozen, it can't absorb much moisture.

In 1851 nearly 75 inches (191 cm) of rain fell, more than double the state's average rainfall. Floods destroyed crops, homes, and businesses. The state also experienced major floods in 1993 and 2008. The flood

PERSPECTIVES

2020 DERECHO

In August 2020 a derecho tore through Iowa. Derechos are storms that bring high winds and heavy rain. This derecho brought winds of up to 140 miles per hour (225 km/h). It was the most expensive thunderstorm disaster in US history. It caused more than $7 billion in damage. Many homes and buildings were damaged or destroyed, along with millions of acres of crops. Some people were without power for more than a week after the storm. Volunteers came to help with cleanup. Pete Martin of North Liberty said, "People are just coming together and helping each other out, so it's kind of the way it is around here."

of 1993 is considered one of the worst natural disasters in the state's history.

Melting snow, extreme rain, and climate change caused more flooding in 2019. Climate change is the warming of Earth's temperatures caused by human activity. Warmer temperatures can lead to heavier rainfalls and more extreme storms, increasing the risk for flooding.

STRAIGHT TO THE
SOURCE

Kirk Larsen is a professor of biology at Luther College. The college is home to the Anderson Prairie, which students use to study prairie restoration and plant diversity. Larsen said of the prairie:

> At 24.7 acres [10 ha], Anderson Prairie is just a postage stamp in a sea of lawns, fields, woods, buildings, and roads, yet this small prairie supports plant and animal biodiversity, provides significant ecosystem services to the community such as pollination, absorbs runoff during rain events, and [removes] atmospheric carbon dioxide which otherwise would contribute to climate change.

> Source: Kirk Larsen. "The Role of Anderson Prairie in Our Educational Mission." *Agora*, vol. 29, no. 2, Spring 2017, pp. 10–14, luther.edu. Accessed 22 Apr. 2021.

CONSIDER YOUR AUDIENCE

Adapt this passage for a different audience, such as your principal or friends. Write a blog post conveying this same information for the new audience. How does your post differ from the original text and why?

RESOURCES AND ECONOMY

D uring the 1900s, Iowa's economy grew. Much of the state's economy depended on agriculture. Corn became the most important crop. But the number of US farms decreased sharply beginning in the 1940s. Instead, a smaller group of people owned a few large farms. Meanwhile, Iowa's cities grew. Many people got jobs in factories and banks. Iowa became known for having excellent schools too.

Approximately 14 percent of the soybeans grown in the United States come from Iowa.

LITERATURE IN IOWA CITY

The University of Iowa is home to the Iowa Writers' Workshop. It was the first creative writing degree program in the country. Many award-winning writers have graduated from the Iowa Writers' Workshop. In 2008 the United Nations Educational, Scientific and Cultural Organization (UNESCO) named Iowa City a UNESCO City of Literature. This honor is given to cities that have contributed to the world of literature. Iowa City was the third city in the world and first in the United States to receive this title.

Today Iowa is the second-most productive agricultural state after California. Iowa produces the most corn, soybeans, and hogs of any US state. Iowa has more hogs than people. The state was home to 24.6 million hogs but just under 3.2 million people in 2020.

ENERGY AND FACTORIES

Renewable energy and manufacturing are two other big industries. Iowa's abundance of corn makes the state

In 2019 wind energy made up more than 40 percent of Iowa's overall electricity.

one of the top ethanol producers in the country. Ethanol is a type of fuel made from plants, including corn. It is more environmentally friendly than regular gasoline. Iowa is also a national leader in wind energy. Its flat, open landscape has room for large wind turbines. Solar power is also gaining popularity in Iowa.

More than 14 percent of Iowa's workforce held manufacturing jobs in 2018. These included jobs that produce foods and beverages, electronics, and vehicles. John Deere is a famous manufacturer in Iowa. It makes agricultural equipment. Its factories provide jobs for thousands of workers. Iowa also makes home appliances and rolled aluminum. Collins Aerospace is the largest employer in Cedar Rapids. This manufacturing company produces parts for commercial and military aircraft.

Health care is another major industry in Iowa. More than 76,000 employees work in Iowa hospitals. In addition some Iowa factories help produce medicines and drugs. Approximately 7 percent of manufacturing jobs in Iowa are related to medicines.

EXPLORE ONLINE

Chapter Four discusses the role of renewable energy in Iowa's economy. The website below goes into more depth about this topic. Does the website answer your questions about renewable energy? Did you learn new information from the website?

WHAT IS RENEWABLE ENERGY?
abdocorelibrary.com/iowa

PEOPLE AND PLACES

Iowa's culture is a blend of urban and rural life. Despite all the state's farmland, most Iowans live in cities. Approximately 65 percent of Iowans live in urban areas, and only 35 percent live in rural areas.

Eighty-five percent of Iowa's population is non-Hispanic white. Hispanic and Latino people make up 6 percent of Iowa's population and Black people 4 percent. Approximately 2 percent are Asian, and American Indians make up 0.4 percent.

Approximately 214,000 people live in Des Moines.

Before becoming president, Herbert Hoover was an engineer and humanitarian who helped war-torn countries.

The Meskwaki settlement in Tama County has grown since its purchase in 1857. It now measures more than 8,100 acres (3,280 ha). The Meskwaki Nation, officially recognized as the Sac and Fox Tribe of the Mississippi in Iowa, is the only federally recognized tribe in the state.

FAMOUS IOWANS

Herbert Hoover was the thirty-first US president (1929–1933). He was born in West Branch in 1874. The Herbert Hoover National Historic Site in West Branch features his childhood home and the Herbert Hoover

Presidential Library and Museum. Hoover and his wife, Lou Henry Hoover, are buried there.

Iowa is home to several famous actors. One is Jason Momoa. Momoa is known for his role in *Aquaman*. He was born in Hawaii and raised in Norwalk, which is near Des Moines. He still visits his family there.

NOTABLE PLACES

Iowa City was Iowa's first state capital. The capital was moved to Des Moines in 1857 because of the city's

PERSPECTIVES
OLYMPIC LEGENDS

Liang Chow is a gymnastics coach. He opened a gym in Des Moines in 1998. He has coached famous gymnasts such as Shawn Johnson and Gabby Douglas. He began coaching Johnson when she was six years old. Johnson won four medals at the 2008 Olympics. She said, "I think I can be proud to say I kind of helped put Iowa out there on the map, which is really exciting for me. I grew up telling everybody I'm from Iowa, and they would always say, 'Where's that? What's in Iowa?' And I always thought it was the greatest place in the world."

more central location. The Old Capitol building in Iowa City is now part of the University of Iowa campus.

IOWA IN THE MOVIES

Iowa has been the setting of several major movies. The 1989 baseball film *Field of Dreams* is one of the most famous. It's about a man who builds a baseball diamond on his farm. Major League Baseball played its first game at the site in 2021. Another Iowa baseball movie came out in 2007. *The Final Season* is about an Iowa high school baseball team. Much of the film was shot in Cedar Rapids, with locals appearing as extras. *The Bridges of Madison County* (1995) stars Meryl Streep. The story was made into a Broadway musical in 2014.

Nearby Riverside has a futuristic claim to fame. Iowa was named in the Star Trek franchise as the birthplace of fictional character Captain James T. Kirk. Riverside claimed the identity of the "Future Birthplace of James T. Kirk" with a plaque. The city is home to a Star Trek museum, the annual TrekFest celebration, and a bronze statue of the captain.

Pikes Peak State Park is just one of Iowa's many natural attractions.

Keokuk is a city in southeastern Iowa. It is known worldwide for its geodes, the state rock. Geodes are rocks with crystals formed inside.

More than 170 farmers markets happen across Iowa. The farmers market in Des Moines is open on Saturdays from May to October. It is one of the busiest in the nation. Approximately 20,000 people come to it every week.

Altoona is home to an amusement park and water park. Sioux City hosts Saturday in the Park. This outdoor music festival is one of the biggest in the Upper Midwest.

People enjoy sports, art, theater, and music throughout the state. Iowans also enjoy getting outdoors. People can see beautiful fall colors along the Mississippi River at Pikes Peak State Park. They can visit Iowa's oldest state park, Backbone State Park, or the Maquoketa Caves. Iowans can go boating at Lake Okoboji or Lake Macbride. For both visitors and residents, Iowa has lots to offer.

STRAIGHT TO THE
SOURCE

Actor Ashton Kutcher was born and raised in Iowa. In 2017 he was awarded the Robert D. Ray Pillar of Character Award from Drake University for his charity work. In his acceptance speech, he talked about what his home state means to him:

> *I left Iowa wanting to get out of Iowa, and the older I get, the more I want to come home. . . . In part, because the more places I go, the more I realize how great it is here, and the more I realize that I almost owe everything of who I am to where I come from. . . . There's an earnestness and an honestness here that lacks in a lot of other places in the world.*

> Source: Matthew Leimkuehler. "Ashton Kutcher on Iowa: 'The More Places I Go, the More I Realize How Great It Is Here.'" *Des Moines Register*, 8 Apr. 2017, desmoinesregister.com. Accessed 26 Apr. 2021.

WHAT'S THE BIG IDEA?

Take a close look at this passage. How does Kutcher view his home state? What traits does he value about Iowa?

IMPORTANT DATES

8,500 years ago
Paleo-Indians build the first permanent settlements in Iowa.

1803
The United States purchases land that includes present-day Iowa from France in the Louisiana Purchase.

1831
The Sauk and the Meskwaki sign a treaty that moves them entirely into Iowa.

1846
Iowa becomes a state on December 28.

1857
The Meskwaki Nation buys a piece of Iowa land on July 13.

1869
Arabella Mansfield, born near Burlington, becomes the first female lawyer in the United States.

1975
Iowa's government makes laws to protect wildlife and help wetlands and prairies recover.

1993
Iowa experiences major flooding, the worst in state history.

2008
Iowa City is designated a UNESCO City of Literature.

STOP AND THINK

Tell the Tale

Chapter One of this book discusses a trip to the Iowa State Fair. Imagine you are going to the Iowa State Fair. Write 200 words about the things you see. What foods do you eat?

Say What?

Studying the geography and cultures of Iowa can mean learning a lot of new vocabulary. Find five words in this book you've never heard before. Use a dictionary to find out what they mean. Then write the meanings in your own words and use each word in a new sentence.

Why Do I Care?

Maybe you are not from an area with wind turbines and solar panels. But that doesn't mean you can't think about the importance of renewable energy. Why is it important to use nature to produce energy? How is Iowa's landscape suited to this energy?

Another View

This book talks about agriculture in Iowa. As you know, every source is different. Ask a librarian or another adult to help you find another source about this topic. Write a short essay comparing and contrasting the new source's point of view with that of this book's author. What is the point of view of each author? How are they similar and why? How are they different and why?

GLOSSARY

aerospace
a science related to the skies and outer space

agriculture
the practice of farming crops and livestock

ancestor
a family member from the past

bluff
a steep bank along a body of water

candidate
a person running for political office

invertebrate
an animal without a backbone

migrate
to move to a different location, usually as the seasons change

territory
an area of land that is not a state but is still controlled by a country

treaty
an official agreement between governments

ONLINE RESOURCES

To learn more about Iowa, visit our free resource websites below.

Core Library
CONNECTION
FREE! COMMON CORE MULTIMEDIA RESOURCES

Visit **abdocorelibrary.com** or scan this QR code for free Common Core resources for teachers and students, including vetted activities, multimedia, and booklinks, for deeper subject comprehension.

Booklinks
NONFICTION NETWORK
FREE! ONLINE NONFICTION RESOURCES

Visit **abdobooklinks.com** or scan this QR code for free additional online weblinks for further learning. These links are routinely monitored and updated to provide the most current information available.

LEARN MORE

Gagne, Tammy. *Exploring the Midwest*. Abdo, 2018.

Lowe, Alexander. *Iowa Hawkeyes*. Weigl, 2020.

INDEX

About the Author

Elaine Hadley grew up in eastern Iowa and still visits her family there often. To her, the best food in the world is fresh Iowa sweet corn in the summer. She now lives in Minnesota, where she enjoys spending time outside and playing board games with her friends.